GERMS

DISEASE-CAUSING ORGANISMS™

W9-AXV-392

BACTERIA

MARGAUX BAUM and LESLI J. FAVOR

rosen publishing's
rosen central®

Published in 2017 by The Rosen Publishing Group, Inc.
29 East 21st Street, New York, NY 10010

Copyright © 2017 by The Rosen Publishing Group, Inc.

First Edition

Library of Congress Cataloging-in-Publication Data

Names: Baum, Margaux, author. | Favor, Lesli J., author.
Title: Bacteria / Margaux Baum and Lesli J. Favor.
Description: First edition. | New York : Rosen Central, 2017. | Series:
 Germs: disease causing organisms | Audience: Grades 5-8. | Includes
 bibliographical references and index.
Identifiers: LCCN 2016002005| ISBN 9781477788387 (library bound) | ISBN
 9781477788363 (pbk.) | ISBN 9781477788370 (6-pack)
Subjects: LCSH: Bacteria--Juvenile literature.
Classification: LCC QR74.8 .F382 2017 | DDC 579.3--dc23
LC record available at http://lccn.loc.gov/2016002005

Manufactured in China

CONTENTS

INTRODUCTION

All around us—in the air, in the water, and even below Earth's surface—there exists a large subset of life, mostly unseen, that scientists believe are likely the most numerous of all living beings on Earth. Their life cycles are finely attuned to the creatures and environment around them, and they affect humanity and other living things in complex ways. They are essential to our life processes, even as some of their number remain dangerous and even potentially fatal in many cases.

The study of bacteria, or bacteriology, has fascinated specialists and humanity at large for millennia. Bacteriologists and other scientists theorize that bacteria have existed on Earth for around 3.5 billion years, long before humanity or its recognizable ancestors showed up. Ancient types of bacteria called archaebacteria, largely unchanged since the early history of the planet, continue to live deep in the ocean adjacent to the hot vents of underwater volcanic zones.

Most bacteria are invisible to the naked due to their extremely small size. Their existence was nearly impossible to prove for sure until technology had improved and allowed human beings to observe tiny things through lenses that could magnify their subjects many times over.

This is what happened when Antonie van Leeuwenhoek (1632–1723) of the Netherlands used homemade lenses to observe water drops. He was amazed to discover a tiny world teeming with life. He called the creatures he saw "animalcules" and sketched their likenesses. He also took samples from his teeth, other water samples (like pond water, rain, and well water), and samples from other parts of the body, and discovered similar organisms. He eventually theorized that such animalcules could be transported by dust in the air.

Despite these discoveries, Leeuwenhoek failed to make the connection that future generations would discover: the link between these microscopic beings and human and animal diseases. At the time, it was believed that parasites and other creatures that grew from decomposing organic matter—such as maggots—appeared spontaneously from meat and human corpses. This theory, known as spontaneous generation, would eventually be replaced as humanity learned more about microscopic organisms.

Bacteria are everywhere—in the human body and the bodies of other living organisms. They live in dirt, in the air, and in water. Some types of bacteria even exist in hot springs, in snow and ice, or in frozen soil, and in the salty seas and oceans. Still others live high in the upper atmosphere.

Though it is a simple single-celled microscopic organism, the bacterium lives a life that is far from simple. Because of the functions bacteria perform in the human body, they are closely involved in every aspect of every human's life. We'll begin with an overview of this tiny creature, from its cell structure to its sizes and shapes. Then we'll describe how bacteria live and their role in causing disease. Finally, we'll look at some beneficial bacteria and the ways in which they are used to enhance life and preserve the environment.

CHAPTER 1

DISCOVERING BACTERIA

After Van Leeuwenhoek and his contemporaries began observing microorganisms, it was a while before advances truly gave humanity a better understanding of the bacterial roots of disease. It was in the 1860s that science took the next big leap in understanding disease. French chemist and microbiologist Louis Pasteur (1822–1895) provided the first major proof that germs cause disease. In further research, Pasteur developed a process, now called pasteurization, to destroy microorganisms in foods and drinks, making them safe to consume. He also experimented with immunizing and vaccinating animals against diseases. Around the same time, in the 1870s and 1880s, German physician Robert Koch identified the anthrax life cycle and identified the bacteria responsible for tuberculosis and cholera.

Indeed, some of history's most horrific plagues and epidemics originated with bacteria. Leprosy, tuberculosis, and diphtheria are all bacterial diseases. The black death that wiped out roughly a third of Europe's population in the fourteenth century was caused by the bacterium *Yersinia pestis*. Another *Yersinia pestis* epidemic swept China in the mid-nineteenth century, and in the first decade of the 1900s, it killed 10 million people in India.

The *Vibrio cholerae* bacterium has caused at least half a dozen pandemics since 1784. A pandemic is an outbreak of a disease that affects a wide geographic area and very large populations. In 1784 in northern India, cholera killed twenty thousand pilgrims at Hardwar, a holy place. During the 1800s, cholera pandemics struck other regions of India, England, France, and Egypt.

WHAT ARE BACTERIA?

Bacteria are classified as part of the kingdom Monera. Organisms in this kingdom have simple cell structures, and most of them are microscopic, meaning they cannot be seen with the naked eye. Besides bacteria, also called eubacteria, Monera include archaebacteria and cyanobacteria. Cyanobacteria were formerly called blue-green algae, but scientists recategorized them after discovering they were more similar to bacteria than to algae.

CELLULAR STRUCTURE

Each bacterium is formed of only one cell, which has a very simple structure. Regular cells have a cell wall surrounding a cell's cytoplasm, and inside the cytoplasm are organelles and a nucleus containing genetic material. Bacteria lack this complex internal structure. All cellular matter floats freely within the cell. A few kinds of bacteria even lack cell walls.

Bacteria, like other members of the kingdom Monera, are prokaryotes. This means that the bacteria do not have a distinct nucleus. Regular cells with nuclei and other organelles like mitochondria are called eukaryotes and are considered a later evolutionary development. In contrast, the DNA (its genetic material), rather than being contained in a nucleus, floats freely within the cell.

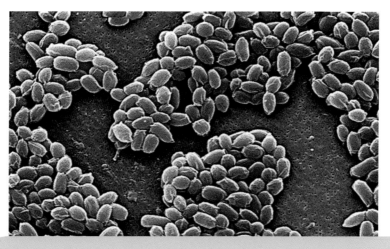

This scanning electron micrograph (SEM) shows *Bacillus anthracis* spores (of the Sterne strain) magnified at about 12,438 times their actual size. This bacteria causes the potentially fatal anthrax infection.

MEASURING THE SIZE OF BACTERIA

Bacteria are microscopic—so tiny that millions could fit on the head of a pin. A fingernail, for instance, may have tens of thousands of bacteria on its surface. The period at the end of this sentence has plenty of surface area for ten thousand of these microbes. The rare exception, a so-called huge bacterium found on the ocean bottom near Namibia in Africa, is about the size of the period at the end of this sentence. Scientists were amazed to find this, the first known bacterium visible with the naked eye.

A unit of measurement called a micrometer, or micron, is used to measure bacteria. Twenty-five thousand microns equal 1 inch (2.5 centimeters). Some of the smallest bacteria are only 1/2 micron in length. It would take 50,000 of them to make a line 1 inch (2.5 cm) long. Most bacteria are between 1 and 5 microns in size. The rare bacteria found off the coast of Namibia can grow up to 500 microns long, a length equaling about 0.02 inch (0.5 millimeter).

BACTERIA

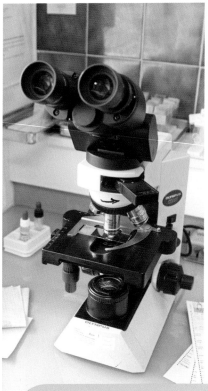

This microscope is used in an analytic laboratory focused on bacteriology in Rambouillet Hospital in Rambouillet, France. Such tools are among the most important in the study (and fight against) bacteria.

SHAPE AND MOVEMENT OF BACTERIA

Bacteria are grouped into three types of cell shapes: spherical, rodlike, and spiral. Coccus cells are spherical. Certain types of cocci cause strep throat and pneumonia, while other types live harmlessly within humans. Bacillus cells are the rodlike cylindrical tubes. Bacilli can cause tuberculosis and anthrax, among other diseases. Spirillum cells have a loose spiral shape. Also called spirochetes, they can cause Lyme disease and other infections.

Most bacteria are single-celled. But sometimes bacteria stick together as pairs, clusters, or lines of cells. When clinging together as a pair, they are called diplo. For example, a stuck-together pair of coccus bacteria are called diplococcus. *Diplococcus pneumoniae* is one cause of conjunctivitis, an eye inflammation. When clustering together, they are called staphylo. Staphylococcus bacteria cause staph infections, meningitis, food poisoning, and other ailments. When linked in chains, they are called strepto. Streptococci, for example, are chains of coccus bacteria. Looking much like strings of beads, they cause strep throat, scarlet fever, sinusitis, and other infections.

Some bacteria move themselves, but others are passengers of the substance in which they live. The mobile ones vary in their capabilities. A slimy bacterium can slide slowly using its own slippery coating. Those with flagella, which are long, whiplike extensions, propel themselves forward in a swimming movement. Spirochetes use structures similar to flagella, located beneath the surface of the cell membrane, to swim. When sensing danger such as a toxic chemical, bacteria evade it. When sensing food, hungry bacteria approach it. Other bacteria, though immobile on their own, may float through the air on a speck of dust or on an insect, hurl through the air in the droplets of a sneeze, or ride along on the skin of an animal.

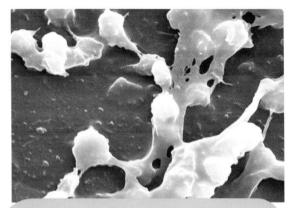

An SEM image of *Staphylococcus aureus* bacteria is magnified here by 2,363 times. About 30 percent of people carry it, most of them harmlessly, but it can be damaging and fatal in health care settings.

BACTERIAL REPRODUCTION

Bacteria are present all over the earth in such great numbers because of their ability to reproduce rapidly. In a process called binary fission, a bacterium splits in two. Each half then splits in two, and those four parts each split in two. The cell division continues, limited only by available space and nutrients. This is called asexual reproduction. The original cell is the mother, and the two resulting ones are daughter cells. Originally half the mother's size, the daughters grow.

In favorable conditions, one bacterium can divide as often as once every twenty minutes. For example, starting with one bacterium at twelve o'clock, you would have two at 12:20, four at 12:40, and eight at 1:00. Bacteria, of course, are plentiful. The tip of a finger might hold 10,000 bacteria at 12:00; by 12:20, there are 20,000 bacteria. By 12:40 there are 40,000 bacteria, and at 1:00 there are 80,000. If humans multiplied on this scale, a family of four would be a family of thirty-two in one hour. More commonly, bacteria divide once every two or three hours and others only once every sixteen hours.

While most bacteria grow through binary fission, some grow through conjugation, a sexual process. In conjugation, two bacteria join and exchange DNA before pulling back apart. While cells produced by fission are identical to the mother— they are clones—those produced by conjugation share DNA from both parents. They are unique.

Occasionally a mutant bacterium arises. It has DNA slightly different from the parent cell's DNA. Consequently, the mutant may survive conditions that would kill its parents. Researchers believe that mutation is responsible for bacteria's ability to adapt to such a wide array of living conditions, both now and throughout the microbes' long history.

Other researchers say it is difficult to prove that mutations arise directly due to certain living conditions. Rather, some believe that random mutations are more common, and that natural selection (the process by which the stronger thrive and the weaker and less adaptable decline) then picks the more hearty candidates.

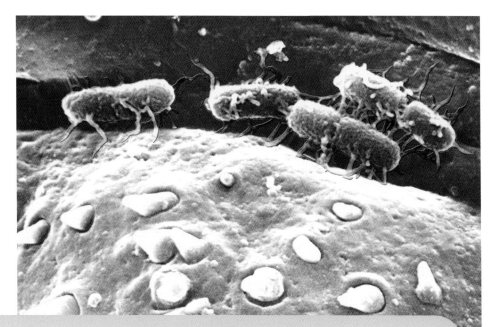

Several *Salmonella typhi* bacteria are shown latching on to the surface of *Schistosoma mansoni*, a parasitic worm that afflicts humans. The former causes the life-threatening illness called typhoid fever.

CHAPTER 2

BACTERIAL LIFE CYCLES

Bacteria vary in their life spans. Some live for merely a few minutes, while others survive for hours. Because of these short spans of times, they maintain their populations and presence through reproduction. They seek and stay in environments that are favorable to their needs, where they can procure nutrients, and stay out of the way of predators and enemies. All the while, the life processes of bacteria go on, many of which are harmful to human health, while others are actually essential to human well-being and life itself.

BACTERIAL HABITATS

Bacteria live everywhere—in more environments and habitats than any other kind of living thing. Saltwater, fresh water, sand, dirt, animals, humans, plants, air, rotting flesh—these are all desirable habitats for bacteria of all kinds. Scientists studying rocks and dirt in mines 1,300 feet (390 meters) deep in the earth found bacteria there. Others studying air 19 miles (30 kilometers) above the earth's surface find bacteria there, too. Some bacteria survive freezing or boiling that would kill other living things. Some types, called anaerobes, thrive in places with no air. They obtain oxygen from their food. Others called aerobes rely on oxygen-rich air for survival, much like humans and animals. Still others can survive either with or without air.

A few kinds of bacteria form spores. A spore is a resting stage, making it possible for the cell to survive adverse conditions. Some spores survive in boiling water for hours, while others survive chemical poisons. Other types of spores endure extreme cold or dehydration. With their tough, dry coats, some spores have survived for hundreds of years. The ruins of Rome have yielded spores nearly 2,000 years old. Other spores have lasted longer. Off the coast of California, in the sediment of the Pacific Ocean, spores were found from 5,800 years ago. In Minnesota's Elk Lake, sediment yielded spores believed to be the oldest ever found, at around 7,000 years old.

Sewage spills are a common cause of beach closures, like this one on Venice Beach in Los Angeles in August 2006. Such spills may sicken as many as 1.5 million Californians annually.

BACTERIA

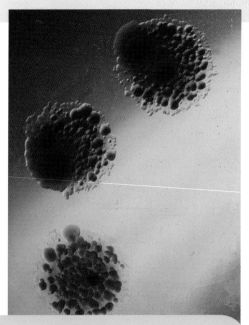

These splotches are clusters of week-old colony samples of *Escherichia coli* (*E. coli*), a bacterium with both positive and negative impacts on human digestive processes and general health.

When a spore encounters favorable living conditions once again, the tough coat gives way to a healthy cell wall. The bacterium resumes normal, active life. Moisture, warmth, and nutrients are conditions favorable to reactivating a dormant bacterium.

Certain bacteria live in the rumens, a stomach section in some animals. Here they help break down cellulose, the stiff matter in plants, during digestion. Without the aid of these bacteria, cows, sheep, goats, and other animals would receive little nutrition from the green plants they graze on. Humans, too, rely on bacteria to help digest food. Colonies of *Escherichia coli* thrive in the intestines, helping to break down food and release nutrients in usable form for the human body.

The human mouth is a bacterium's paradise. Warm and moist, it provides an ideal habitat for billions of bacteria. Sugars and starches in food pass through the mouth, feeding the bacteria as well as their host. Colonies of the microbes live on the tongue, teeth, and gums, in crevices between teeth, and in dental plaque.

Most of these mouth microbes are harmless. Some are beneficial, while others can do damage. For instance, unbrushed teeth allow bacteria to grow and produce sufficient acid to cause tooth decay. The longer the bacteria colonize the tooth, the deeper into the tooth their acid eats, first through the enamel, then through the dentin of the tooth, and finally into its soft, pulpy center. If bacteria cause this much damage to a tooth, it likely will need to be pulled out by a dentist. In a similar fashion, gums in an untended mouth multiply bacteria that cause gum disease.

NUTRITIONAL NEEDS

Bacteria need nutrients to survive, just like people do. The bacterium takes in food through the cell wall. First, the bacterium secretes enzymes from the cell wall onto food outside. The enzymes break down the food into soluble form. Being soluble

Spirillum volutans, shown here, is usually found in stagnant freshwater and saltwater environments full of organic material, where it feeds on dead and rotting tissue.

means the food can dissolve in a liquid, and in this form the bacterium absorbs the food through its cell wall. Inside the cell, enzymes further process the food.

BACTERIA

For some bacteria, mineral compounds provide the best nutrients. Using sulfur, minerals in water, and carbon dioxide from air, these bacteria manufacture carbohydrates, fats, proteins, and vitamins. Because they create their own nourishment, they are called autotrophic, or self-nourishing. Other bacteria need more complex foods. Parasitic bacteria depend on a living host to provide nourishment. Bacteria called saprophytes feast on rotting animal carcasses, dead bugs, and other types of decaying flesh.

Just as plants use photosynthesis to manufacture nutrients, so do some anaerobic bacteria. These bacteria contain substances that capture energy from sunlight and use it to make food. Whereas plants produce oxygen as a waste product, anaerobic bacteria do not. Cyanobacteria also employ photosynthesis, and these do give off oxygen as waste.

After digestion, the bacterium expels waste matter through the cell wall. The waste products of bacteria that are poisonous to other living things are called toxins.

A NATURAL BALANCE

One of bacteria's valuable roles in nature is to assist in the decay of dead organisms. Along with earthworms and fungi, bacteria break down organic matter such as fallen leaves, dead plants and wood, and animal carcasses. Bacteria work during the final stages of decomposition, after earthworms and fungi have broken the matter into tiny pieces. As they feast on organic molecules, bacteria break them down into basic elements, including nitrates, minerals, water, and carbon dioxide. They release these elements back into the soil and air, where they origi-nated. Thus enriched, the soil and atmosphere can support a new cycle of life. If it weren't for decomposition from bacteria, dead organic matter would pile up, tying up the basic elements needed for new life. Eventually, all life on earth would die out.

Another process involves breaking down solid waste from humans and animals. In breaking down manure, for example, bacteria release nitrogen, phosphorus, and potassium, important nutri-ents in fertile soil. For this rea-son, decaying manure is used as a soil fertilizer. Billions of pounds of waste are produced daily worldwide. Without the steady work of bacteria, aided by other microbes including fungi and protozoa, waste would make Earth unlivable.

The rounded nodules shown on these roots are produced by rhizobium bacteria. These bacteria make their home in plants, which in turn benefit from the bacteria's ability to fix nitrogen.

BACTERIA AND NITROGEN

In septic tanks, anaerobic bacteria break down human waste. One byproduct of this is gas, mainly methane, which can be trapped and utilized as fuel. The remaining solid matter can be used as a fertilizer. On a larger scale, bacteria help treat the sewage of huge cities. At sewage plants, huge beds of gravel are sprayed with sewage. On the gravel is a film formed of aerobic bacteria and other microbes. These microorganisms break down the waste.

In a process called nitrogen fixation, bacteria in the soil help green plants thrive by making nitrogen accessible. In its gaseous form, nitrogen makes up nearly 80 percent of the air. However, green plants cannot use nitrogen in the gaseous form. They depend on bacteria that take in nitrogen to fuel their own growth. Bacteria such as azotobacter use nitrogen gas to form nitrates and ammonia, compounds that plants use to fuel their growth. Other bacteria called rhizobia live in nodules (swellings) on the roots of legumes such as peas, beans, and clover. In this symbiotic relationship, both the microbe and the plant benefit. From the plant the bacteria obtains food, and from the bacteria the plant obtains nitrogen compounds.

The bacterium's role as an agent of decay is crucial in maintaining the natural balance of life itself. Bacterial processes help introduce valuable nutrients into the soil and carbon dioxide into the air, thus benefiting plant life and, by extension, animal life, too. The role of bacteria is not limited to these spheres, however. Their roles in both food production and in disease make them crucial in life or death matters for human populations around the world, as well as for plants and animals, too.

CHAPTER 3

THE PERILS OF BACTERIA

One reason that many foods need to be washed and prepared carefully is due to the prevalence of bacteria. Improper food preparation, including undercooking, can lead to varying degrees of sickness, typically called food poisoning. Some bacteria make food inedible or harmful because they spoil. At the same time, bacteria are used in many ancient as well as industrial food processes that create healthy and tasty food products, including yogurt and many types of cheese.

Bacteria active in the decay process are responsible for food spoilage. Moderate temperatures and some moisture are ideal for bacteria to thrive in many types of food. However, refrigeration helps slow spoilage, and freezing can halt spoilage, at least until the food is thawed. At this time, the bacteria become active again. Heat used in cooking and baking kills many types of bacteria.

In certain foods, bacteria bring about spoilage more readily than in others. A cheesy slice of pizza left sitting on a kitchen counter will spoil much faster than a piece of dry toast. A glass of milk left out on the counter will sour more quickly than a glass of sugary, acidic lemonade. A can of salt, a box of sugar cubes, a bag of flour, and a box of dry breakfast cereal are all examples of foods that do not readily support bacterial growth.

On the other hand, meats, cheeses, and prepared foods are hospitable to bacterial growth, due in part to their moisture content. In general, most types of bacteria do not grow in dry or salty foods. For this reason, drying and salting are effective methods of food preservation. Similarly, very sugary foods are not conducive to bacterial growth, nor are acidic foods such as vinegar.

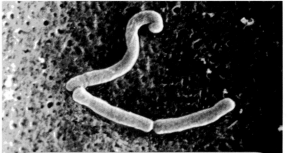

Lactobacillus (pictured) is a bacteria found in many dairy products and a major part of the lactic acid bacteria group. Lactobacilli can be used to treat diarrhea and to prevent digestive disorders following a patient's antibiotic regimen.

Special care must be taken when canning foods. In the canning process, foods are heated to kill bacteria and then sealed in sterile jars or cans. Thus prepared, foods can be stored without refrigeration or freezing for many months. However, some spores and heat-tolerant bacteria called thermophilic bacteria survive high temperatures. If sufficient heat is not used for the proper length of time, the microbes survive. They grow in the canned food or become active when the container is opened.

Botulin, a poisonous bacterial waste product, causes botulism. Even in tiny amounts, the toxin attacks the human nervous system and can be fatal. Botulin comes from a spore that survives boiling water for up to five hours. Home-canned foods are most susceptible to botulin. Superheated with steam, commercially canned foods are less likely to carry the toxin. Whatever its origin, an unopened jar whose suction seal has popped up or a swollen can is likely to contain botulin.

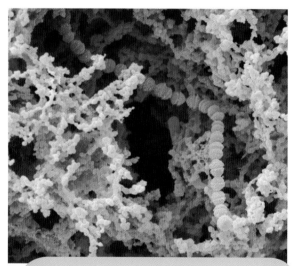

These bacteria—*Lactobacillus bulgaricus* (colored orange) and *Lactococcus* (colored blue)—work to coagulate milk, producing yogurt, and are generally beneficial to human health.

PASTEURIZATION

Pasteurization is a method of killing harmful bacteria in fresh dairy products such as milk and cream. Milk bottled for sale to the public is pasteurized, as are half-and-half and cream. One method of pasteurizing fresh milk is to heat it for thirty minutes at 145° Fahrenheit (63° Celsius). A quicker method of killing the bacteria is to heat it to

161°F (71.6°C) for fifteen seconds. Immediately following both methods of pasteurization, the milk is cooled rapidly to preserve its flavor. Other methods of pasteurization are used for other dairy products.

PROPER HYGIENE COUNTS

Poor hygiene on the part of food handlers can allow bacteria to find their way into the human stomach and wreak havoc there. Bacteria make up a large part of solid human waste, for example, and a person who does not wash up after a trip to the restroom can transfer bacteria to the food he or she touches. The contaminated food can cause stomach pain, vomiting, and diarrhea.

Salmonella, rod-shaped bacteria, live in the intestines of chickens and help the fowls digest their food. When chickens are slaughtered and sold as raw poultry, bacteria can survive on the meat. A cook who does not thoroughly wash his or her hands after handling raw chicken can transfer salmonella to cooked food, clean dishes, or anything else touched afterward. Similarly, the cook must prepare the chicken at a high enough temperature to kill the salmonella. Raw or undercooked eggs are also carriers of salmonella bacteria. Symptoms of poisoning by salmonella include stomach pain, fever, vomiting, and diarrhea.

(continued on the next page)

BACTERIA

(continued from the previous page)

Other types of bacteria invade the intestines when poor hygiene or inadequate cooking allow them to survive on food. Campylobacter, for example, survives on undercooked food. Once in the intestines, this bacteria begins destroying the mucus lining, causing diarrhea. Shigella is a kind of bacteria carried by flies and found on food. Poor sanitation in food preparation can allow shigella to survive and attack the lining of the small intestines. Symptoms include cramps and diarrhea, the body's way of trying to rid itself of the microbe.

PATHOGENS

While some bacterial infections are food-borne, others result when bacteria invade the body by other means. Called pathogens, disease-causing bacteria are responsible for infections ranging from acne to pinkeye to pneumonia. Some pathogens multiply in the body so rapidly that they interfere with the functions of tissues and organs. Others excrete toxins, chemicals that are poisonous to the human body.

The human body has natural defenses against the entry of disease-causing bacteria. On the skin's surface, harmless bacteria live, protecting their turf against invading bacteria. Mucous membranes and tiny hairs in the nose trap bacteria, where they are expelled when the nose is blown. Bacteria entering through the mouth or nose may be killed by mucous membranes in the mouth or throat. Those making their way to the stomach are killed by acids there. Tears in the eyes and saliva in the mouth form additional defenses.

Cuts, scrapes, skin punctures, and animal bites provide pathways for bacteria to enter the body. But even these temporary entryways are protected. When the skin is cut, for example, some of the damaged cells release histamine. This chemical signals the body to send more blood to the injury, and the area swells. The blood clots, sealing the cut. Besides that, white blood cells rush to the injury. Called phagocytes, they eat invading bacteria. Afterward, the phagocytes die, and the mass of dead phagocytes and demolished bacteria remains as pus. Other immune system white cells called lymphocytes produce chemicals to attack and kill bacteria and other invaders. Specific lymphocytes target specific kinds of bacterial invaders.

Despite the body's defenses, some pathogenic microbes find a way in and survive. Once inside the body, the bacteria carry on with the business of living—multiplying, eating, and excreting waste. Infections result when they multiply to numbers great enough to interfere with bodily functions or when their poisonous waste products—toxins—cause damage.

Pneumonia is a respiratory infection resulting from bacteria that multiply rapidly in the lungs. As the lungs become filled with bacteria, the person has increasing difficulty breathing. Eventually the victim can suffocate and die.

BACTERIA

Hemophilus bacteria are mostly harmless, except for *Hemophilus influenzae*, which causes whooping cough and meningitis. Whooping cough, characterized by coughing and vomiting, is highly contagious. Meningitis is an inflammation of the membranes covering the brain and spinal cord. Meningitis is also caused by other bacteria, including meningococcus and various kinds of pneumococci, streptococci, and staphylococci. Most frequently, children under the age of ten suffer from the disease. Early diagnosis is vital since brain damage and death may result.

A soil bacterium, *Clostridium tetani*, lurks in spore form, entering scratches or puncture wounds that are contaminated with dirt. Once in the wound, the spore is activated by rotting tissue. It releases a toxin that enters the nervous system and spinal cord, causing tetanus. Also known as lockjaw, a tetanus infection causes severe, uncontrollable muscle contractions. Spasms of the jaw muscles give the disease its nickname. The disease can be fatal, though it is preventable with a vaccine.

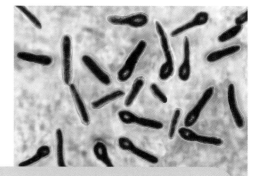

The list of bacterial infections goes on. Streptococcus causes scarlet fever. *Mycobacterium bovis* causes tuberculosis. Carried by ticks, *Borrelia burgdorferi* causes Lyme disease. *Rickettsia* cause typhus and spotted fever. The

These *Clostridium tetani* bacteria cause the illness called tetanus. Even a minor infection (such as from a rusty nail piercing one's toe) can lead to production of tetanospasmin, a poison toxic to the human nervous system.

Chlamydia trachomatis bacterium causes chlamydia, a sexually transmitted disease that can result in the inability to have children. Leprosy, more common in centuries past but still present today, results from *Mycobacterium leprae. Legionella pneumophila* bacteria cause Legionnaire's disease, a kind of pneumonia. Found in refrigerated foods such as potato salad and cold cuts, the bacterium *Listeria monocytogenes* causes food poisoning and in some cases death.

Not all pathogens and toxins are life threatening. For instance, acne is a bacterial infection that affects a majority of people, particularly during the teenage years. Oil in the skin clogs the tiny pores of the skin. Bacteria collect and feed on the oil, multiplying until an acne sore results. An increase in the skin's oil production during the teen years makes young people particularly susceptible to acne.

Caused by the *Helicobacter pylori* bacterium, an ulcer is a sore in the lining of the stomach or duodenum, a part of the small intestine. Often called peptic ulcers, these infections can produce symptoms of abdominal pain, nausea, vomiting, bloating, and heartburn. Ulcers are treated with drugs such as antacids and antibiotics.

Commonly called pinkeye, conjunctivitis is an inflammation of transparent membranes in the eyeball and eyelid. The staphylococci, pneumococci, and *Haemophilus influenzae* bacteria cause most cases of bacterial pinkeye, which is highly contagious. Conjunctivitis can also result from allergies, viruses, and other causes.

MAKING VACCINES AND OTHER MEDICINES

The human body produces natural defenses, called antibodies, to fight disease-causing bacteria. To combat the microorganisms' toxins, the body produces antitoxins. Vaccines and antibiotics are manufactured weapons used to prevent or fight infections. These man-made forms of treatment are prepared using bacteria or their poisonous waste. Vaccines and antitoxin injections are preventive, meaning that they are given when no infection is present in order to protect against a future attack. Antibiotics are used to treat infections that have already set in.

Disease-producing bacteria are used to create vaccines that prevent infections. Given as an injection, a vaccine contains dead or weakened bacteria of the sort the vaccine protects against. The dead bacteria stimulate the human body to react as it would to live bacteria—by producing antibodies. These antibodies protect the individual against the specific kind

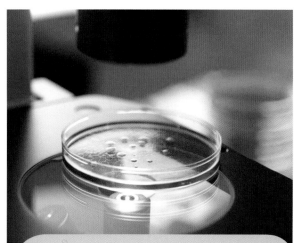

This petri dish contains bacterial cultures being grown by scientists. Many helpful, lifesaving medicines are produced in exactly this way, especially antibiotics and antitoxins.

of bacteria contained in the vaccine. Vaccines protect for a year or longer.

Scientists use bacterial waste products to make antitoxin injections. To make these solutions, the scientist first injects toxins into living animals. The animal's body produces antitoxins in response to the injected toxins. Then the scientist draws blood from the animal, separates out the serum, and uses it to make an antitoxin for use by humans. Antitoxins work more quickly than vaccines, but they don't last as long—only a few weeks or months.

Bacterial infection is often treated using drugs called antibiotics. These are drugs made up of a secretion made by types of bacteria and other microorganisms, which in turn fights bacterial infection. Bacitracin and polymyxin are two well-known antibiotics. Streptomyces, mold-like substances that exist in soil, are a group of bacteria that are utilized to create tetracycline, neomycin, and many other different classes of antibiotics. Among the best known and effective antibiotics is penicillin, which is derived from the mold known as *Penicillium notatum*.

Antibiotics are among the most valuable weapons against pathogens and toxins that break through the body's natural defenses, along with vaccines. Nations that have well developed health systems have access to great amounts of these and have subsequently eliminated many types of infections entirely among their populations.

BACTERIA

One issue that has arisen in recent years, however, has been the growth of bacterial antibiotic resistance. When antibiotics are widely used, the strains of bacteria that resist them will tend to survive more than weaker strains, an evolutionary process that many organisms undergo and that is often referred to as natural selection.

As these stronger strains grow in population, the antibiotics will be less and less effective in treating these bacterial infections. This is why many health professionals recommend not resorting to antibiotics for sicknesses like the common cold or the flu, unless the sufferers are truly very sick. There are fears that antibiotic resistance is growing in both human and animal populations administered antibiotics to make up for widespread illnesses from being raised in very close quarters. Some scientists are also convinced that antibiotic resistance is also passed from animal to human consumers through the meat many people consume.

CHAPTER 4

BENEFICIAL BACTERIA

Plants and animals all suffer from bacterial infections at some point. But harmful bacteria are just one part of the whole picture. Bacteria that are beneficial to human beings exist within their digestive systems, for example. Others are actively used in food production, medicine, and many other beneficial activities. In these ways, bacteria of all kinds also contribute to making human life safer, more hygienic, and even more enjoyable.

BIOPHARMACEUTICALS

Drug makers are always on the lookout for bacteria that may prove useful in fighting diseases, sometimes known in recent years known as "biopharmaceuticals." In pharmaceutical laboratories, "bioprospectors" search for microbes to use in new drugs. Much like miners prospecting for gold, these scientists screen large numbers of microbes in order to locate useful ones. Many lifesaving new drugs result from this tedious work. Some parasitic worm infections can be treated by ivermectin, produced by bacteria that live in soil.

Not all drugs are made by bacteria, of course. Some valuable medicines are created by other organisms in defense against bacteria. For example, a fungus that grows on the Pacific yew tree produces a substance to fight disease-causing bacteria. Scientists found that this drug, called paclitaxel, fights certain kinds of cancer, too.

Many kinds of bacteria develop resistance or immunity to antibiotics that previously killed them. For example, staphylococcus is a common bacterium, responsible for staph infections in hospitals. It has developed a resistance to certain antibiotics. Bacteria's ability to adapt drives scientists to search for newer drugs that will be effective, at least for a time. Viruses known as bacteriophages attack and kill specific bacteria. Scientists are turning to viruses in search of new means of combating bacterial infections. *E. coli* bacteria, for example, fall victim to certain viruses.

One agricultural application of bacteria research is the creation of biological pesticides. *Bacillus thuringiensis* killed this white cabbage butterfly caterpillar, a pest that damages cabbage crops.

The study of bacteria in laboratories results in more than just drugs to fight infections. Bacteria are used to rid crops of pests naturally. Natural pesticides called bioinsecticides repel pests or kill them outright. For instance, the *Bacillus thuringiensis* bacterium kills pests on crops and kills mosquitoes. Harmless to humans, it is a safe alternative to chemical pesticide and is used world-wide. Some bioinsecticides are mixed with cornstarch in a special process that prepares them to be spread on crops by crop-dusting aircraft.

USING BACTERIA TO ADVANCE GENETIC ENGINEERING

Like all living cells, bacteria contain hereditary information. This hereditary information is called deoxyribonucleic acid (DNA). It determines the cell's traits and activities. When the bacterium splits, the DNA determines that the new cells have the same or similar traits as the first cell. DNA is comprised of chromosomes that carry genes. Floating around inside the cell are also small pieces of DNA called plasmids.

Scientists discovered that they could take plasmids from one bacterium and put them into another. This action changed the traits of the altered bacterium. Scientists also found that they could cut up the DNA in the chromosome and join the pieces with DNA from a different kind of bacteria. The new DNA carried some traits from both bacteria. These activities are known as genetic engineering.

Scientists took what they learned from working with bacteria and applied it to other living organisms. Genetic

(continued on the next page)

BACTERIA

(continued from the previous page)

engineers learned how to move genes from one animal to another and even from an animal or human to a plant. They modified fruits and vegetables to produce more desirable strains. In the mid-1980s, they began cloning organisms, making genetic copies of them. Scientists used the fertilized eggs of sheep, cows, rabbits, and other animals to make clones. In early 1997, a sheep named Dolly became famous as the first complex organism cloned from the cell of an adult. This scientific work, which amazed people all over the world, grew out of the original work with bacterial DNA.

INDUSTRIAL USES OF BACTERIA

Besides being important to laboratory research, bacteria are important in real-world applications such as mining. Called biomining, a process using the *Thiobacillus ferrooxidans* bacterium extracts metals from ore. This microbe gets its energy from combining oxygen with inorganic material such as minerals. In doing so, the bacterium releases acid that washes metals out of ore. Miners remove copper from

Bacterial research provided the foundation for later genetic milestones. Without it, scientists would probably not have been able to clone Dolly the sheep, the world's first cloned mammal, pictured here.

ore using *ferrooxidans* bacteria. Gold, too, is separated from ore using biomining.

Thanks to genetic engineering, a kind of bacteria has been developed for the purpose of eating oil. Oil spills like the *Exxon Valdez* spill in 1989 coat huge areas of water with oil. As a result, vast numbers of fish, birds, and other wildlife suffer or die. The 11- million-gallon (41.6-million-liter) *Exxon Valdez* accident created an oil slick covering nearly 100 square miles (260 square km) off the coast of Alaska.

For some bacteria, this oil is a feast. In the early 1970s, scientists genetically created bacteria that could eat oil. To clean up an oil slick, sawdust is sprinkled over it. The oil soaks into the sawdust, forming globs that sink to the bottom. Here bacteria devour the oil, decomposing it and making it harmless. Another method of cleaning an oil slick is sprinkling it with clay. Like the sawdust, the clay absorbs the oil, only it does not sink. Bacteria decompose these clumps of oil-soaked clay.

BACTERIA IN FOOD PRODUCTION

The changes wrought by bacteria in food can be a good thing. Fermentation is the key in the production of many foodstuffs. It is a chemical process brought about by certain microorganisms, including some kinds of bacteria. For example, *Lactobacillus bulgaricus* bacteria change milk sugar into lactic acid, a process that produces buttermilk, cream, and yogurt. So-called live yogurt contains living lactobacilli. A seemingly endless variety of cheeses are

BACTERIA

A technician at Roquefort Société, in Saint–Affrique, France, infuses *Penicillium roqueforti* into a tray of milk to make the well-known Roquefort cheese.

made using different combinations of bacteria, each blend resulting in a different flavor. Other foods and beverages made with the help of bacteria include pickles, soy sauce, sauerkraut, wine, beer, coffee, chocolate, and some cured meats, among others.

Dill pickles, for example, are the end product of fermenting cucumbers. Streptococci bacteria begin the fermentation process, and as the level of acidity of the cucumbers falls, the *leuconostoc* and *pediococcus* species continue the process, helped along by *Lactobacillus plantarum* as well.

Bacteria has a tremendous impact on everyday life for humans and all living beings, as much as any other organism on the planet. Their uses in science, medicine, industry, and our own digestive systems are invaluable. Hence, while everyone should strive to keep their environments clean, their food and water edible and drinkable, they should also realize that "bacteria" need not be a bad word. Instead, they should be studied and celebrated as a vital component of our incredibly complex, interconnected world.

GLOSSARY

AEROBIC Living in the presence of oxygen.

ANAEROBIC Living in the absence of oxygen.

ANTIBIOTIC A drug made to destroy living organisms, such as bacteria, that cause infection.

ANTIBODY A protein produced by white blood cells in an immune response, that is, to fight organisms such as bacteria that cause infection.

ANTITOXIN An antibody produced to fight a toxin.

BACILLUS Singular of "bacilli." A bacterium cell with a rodlike shape.

BACTERIOPHAGE A virus that attacks and kills bacteria.

BACTERIUM Singular of "bacteria." A single-celled, generally microscopic organism in the kingdom Monera that is present on the earth in vast numbers.

BIOPHARMACEUTICAL A medicinal product made from, or extracted from, biological sources, such as bacteria.

CELL The smallest unit of independent life. All living organisms are made up of one or more cells.

CHROMOSOME The DNA-containing particle within a cell.

CLONE An organism that is an exact genetic match to its parent.

COCCUS Singular of "cocci." A bacteria cell with a spherical shape.

CONJUGATION A method of sexual reproduction used by some kinds of bacteria in which genetic information is exchanged.

DNA (DEOXYRIBONUCLEIC ACID) DNA is made up of genes, the hereditary information for a cell.

BACTERIA

EPIDEMIC An outbreak of a disease affecting a large proportion of a population at once.

FISSION Also called binary fission, the reproduction of cells through division. One cell divides into two identical clones.

FLAGELLUM A long, whiplike tail on some protozoans, including some bacteria. Flagella provide a means of movement.

GENE A tiny part of a chromosome that holds hereditary information for a cell.

IMMUNITY Resistance to infection or poison.

MICROBE A microscopic organism. Also called a microorganism or germ.

NITROGEN FIXATION The process whereby certain bacteria in the soil take nitrogen gas from the air and convert it to nitrates, which are necessary to plant growth.

PASTEURIZATION A process whereby liquids or foods are heated to specific temperatures for certain lengths of time to kill microscopic organisms.

PATHOGEN A disease-causing bacterium or other agent.

PLASMID A particle of DNA within a bacterium cell.

SPIRILLUM Singular of "spirilla." A coil-shaped bacterium cell. Cells with this shape are also called spirochetes.

SPORE A resting stage of a bacterium that can withstand harsh conditions in order to survive for long periods of time.

TOXIN Poisonous waste material produced by a bacterium.

VACCINE A solution made from weakened or dead disease-causing organisms (such as bacteria and viruses). Injected into a person, vaccines cause the body to develop antibodies.

FOR MORE INFORMATION

American Public Health Association
800 I Street NW
Washington, DC 2001-3710
(202) 777-2742
comments@apha.org
Website: http://www.apha.org
The American Public Health Association (APHA) is a professional organization for public health practitioners in the United States, championing the health of all people and all communities.

Association of Medical Microbiology and Infectious Disease Canada (AMMI)
192 Bank Street
Ottawa, ON K2P 1W8
Canada
(613) 260-3233
info@ammi.ca
Website: http://www.ammi.ca
The Association of Medical Microbiology and Infectious Disease Canada (AMMI) promotes the prevention, diagnosis, and treatment of human infectious diseases through its involvement in education, research, clinical practice, and patient advocacy.

The Centers for Disease Control and Prevention (CDC)
1600 Clifton Road
Atlanta, GA 30333
(404) 639-3534
(800) 232-4636
Website: http://www.cdc.gov

BACTERIA

The Centers for Disease Control and Prevention (CDC) is the primary United States government agency in charge of tracking, treating, and preventing public health threats, including infectious diseases.

National Institutes of Health (NIH)
9000 Rockville Pike
Bethesda, MD 20892
(301) 496-4000
NIHinfo@od.nih.gov
Website: http://www.nih.gov
The National Institutes of Health (NIH) is a research facility in the Washington, DC, area that is the primary agency of the United States government in charge of biomedical and health-related research.

WEBSITES

Because of the changing nature of Internet links, Rosen Publishing has developed an online list of websites related to the subject of this book. This site is updated regularly. Please use this link to access the list:

http://www.rosenlinks.com/GDCO/bac

FOR FURTHER READING

Biskup, Agnieszka. *The Surprising World of Bacteria with Max Axiom, Super Scientist*. Mankato, MN: Capstone Press, 2010.

Crawford, Dorothy H. *Viruses: A Very Short Introduction*. New York, NY: Oxford University Press, 2011.

Greenhaven Press. *Superbugs* (At Issue). Farmington Hills, MI: Greenhaven Press, 2016.

Guilfoile, Patrick G., Ph.D. *Antibiotic-Resistant Bacteria*. New York, NY: Chelsea House, 2013.

Hollar, Sherman. *A Closer Look at Bacteria, Algae, and Protozoa*. New York, NY: Rosen Publishing, 2011.

Jones, Phill. *Viruses* (Science Foundations). New York, NY: Chelsea House, 2012.

Lemaster, Leslie Jean. *Bacteria and Viruses*. Chicago, IL: Children's Press, 1999.

Markovics, Joyce L. *Tiny Invaders!: Deadly Microorganisms* (Nature's Invaders) Mankato, MN: Capstone Press, 2013.

Parker, Steve. *Cocci, Spirilla & Other Bacteria*. Minneapolis, MN: Compass Point Books, 2009.

Quammen, David. *Spillover: Animal Infections and the Next Human Pandemic*. New York, NY: W. W. Norton, 2013.

Reh, Beth Donovan. *Germs* (Exploring Science and Medical Discoveries). Farmington Hills, MI: Greenhaven Press, 2013.

Rodriguez, A. M. *Edward Jenner: Conqueror of Smallpox* (Great Minds of Science). Berkeley Heights, NJ: Enslow Publishers, 2006.

Roza, Greg. *Bacteria Up Close* (Under the Microscope). New York, NY: Gareth Stevens, 2013.

Wanjie, Anne, ed. *The Basics of Biology* (Core Concepts). New York, NY: Rosen Publishing, 2013.

BACTERIA

Wanjie, Anne, ed. *The Basics of Cell Biology* (Core Concepts). New York, NY: Rosen Publishing, 2013.

Wanjie, Anne, ed. *The Basics of Microbes* (Core Concepts). New York, NY: Rosen Publishing, 2013.

Wearing, Judy. *Staph, Strep, Clostridium, and Other Bacteria* (Class of their Own). St. Catharines, ON, Canada: Crabtree Publishing, 2012.

Willett, Edward. *Infectious Disease Specialists: Hunting Down Disease* (Extreme Science Careers). New York, NY: Enslow Publishing, 2015.

BIBLIOGRAPHY

Biddle, Wayne. *A Field Guide to Germs*. New York, NY: Henry Holt, 1995.

Eberhart-Phillips, Jason. *Outbreak Alert: Responding to the Increasing Threat of Infectious Diseases*. Oakland, CA: New Harbinger Publications, 2000.

Facklam, Howard, and Margery Facklam. *Bacteria*. New York, NY: Twenty-First Century Books, 1994.

Farrell, Jeanette. *Invisible Enemies: Stories of Infectious Disease*. New York, NY: Farrar, Straus & Giroux, 1998.

Patent, Dorothy Hinshaw. *Bacteria: How They Affect Other Living Things*. New York, NY: Holiday House, 1980.

Snedden, Robert. *The Benefits of Bacteria*. Chicago, IL: Heinemann, 2000.

INDEX

ABOUT THE AUTHORS

Margaux Baum is a young adult nonfiction author from Queens, New York. She has written numerous books for Rosen Publishing covering disease prevention, drug addiction, and science.

Lesli J. Favor received her BA in English from the University of Texas at Arlington and then earned her MA and PhD from the University of North Texas. She has also written biographies on people such as Francisco de Coronado and Martin Van Buren. She lives with her husband, Stephen, in Dallas.

PHOTO CREDITS